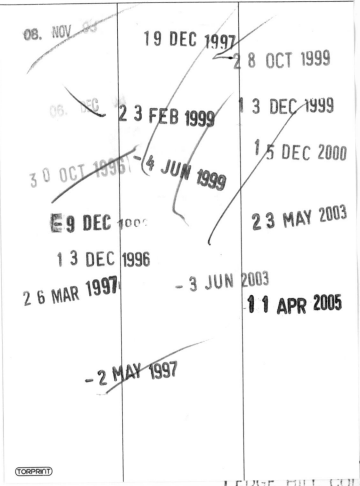

D1337733

Macmillan Education

523291

'For David'

Selection © Moira Andrew 1987
Illustration © Macmillan Education Ltd 1987

First published 1987

Published by
MACMILLAN EDUCATION LTD
Houndmills, Basingstoke, Hampshire RG21 2XS
and London
Companies and representatives
throughout the world

Typeset in Great Britain by
Acorn Bookwork, Salisbury, Wiltshire

Printed in Hong Kong

British Library Cataloguing in Publication Data
Poetry 4: Unicorn and lions.—(Junior
poetry anthologies; 4)
1. English poetry—20th century
I. Andrew, Moira   II. Series
821'.914'08   PR1174
ISBN 0-333-39204-3

Acknowledgements

The editor and publishers wish to thank the following who have kindly given permission for the use of copyright material:

George Allen and Unwin Ltd for 'The Stolen Orange' from **Love Poems** by Brian Patten (1981) and 'You'd Better Believe Him' from **Notes to the Hurrying Man** by Brian Patten. Atheneum Publishers Inc for 'The Chant of the Awakening Bulldozers' from **Catch Me a Wind** by Patricia Hubbell Copyright © (1968). Bloodaxe Books Ltd for 'Flowers', 'January' and 'Finding a Sheep's Skull' from **Collected Poems** by Frances Horovitz (1985). Curtis Brown Ltd on behalf of Christopher Isherwood for 'Camel' from **People one ought to know**, Macmillan (1982). Freda Bromhead for 'Sunset'. Alan Brownjohn for 'Ostrich' from **Brownjohn's Beasts**, Macmillan (1970). Dave Calder for 'giraffe' and 'Elephant'. Laura Cecil on behalf of the James Reeves Estate for 'Waiting' from **James Reeves The Complete Poems** by James Reeves. Chatto & Windus Ltd for 'Barn Owl' from **Mountains, Polecats, Pheasants** by Leslie Norris (1974). Collins Publishers Ltd for 'My Party' from **Rabbiting On** by Kit Wright. John Cotton for 'Uncle Tom' from **The Highfield Write-a-Poem**, The Priopus Press (1982) and 'Party Conversation'. Andre Deutsch for 'This morning my father' from **Mind your own Business** by Michael Rosen (1974). Maura Dooley for 'Early Morning'. Joan Downar for 'Cat-Poem'. Edna Eglinton for 'A Direct Road' and 'In praise of plastic flowers'. Roger Elkin for 'Barn Owl'. Ian Emberson for 'A weed is a flower in the wrong place' from **Doodles in the Margin of my Life**, Fighting Cocks Press (1981). Faber and Faber Ltd for 'Transplanting' from **The Collected Poems of Theodore Roethke** by Theodore Roethke, 'Leaves' and 'There Came a Day' from **Season Songs** by Ted Hughes, 'In watchful community' from **Positives** by Thom Gunn and 'The Play Way' from **Death of a Naturalist** by Seamus Heaney. John Fairfax for 'Shut your Eyes or Turn your Head' and 'Neighbour'. Pam Gidney for 'Figure and Ground', 'Galactic Cat' and 'Phoebus' Palindrome'. Pamela Gillilan for 'Requiem'. David Harmer for 'Where it is always Summer'. David Higham Associates Ltd on behalf of Elizabeth Jennings for 'My Grandmother' from **Collected Poems**, Macmillan, and on behalf of Charles Causley for 'Riley' and 'My mother saw a dancing bear' from **Collected Poems**, Macmillan, 'At Candlemas' from **Figgie Hobbin**, Macmillan and 'Singing Game' from **Secret Destinations**, Macmillan, and on behalf of Clive Sanson for 'School Mistress' from **Dorset Village**, Methuen & Co Ltd. Philip Hosbaum for 'The Astigmatic' from **In Retreat**, Macmillan. The Hogarth Press Ltd for 'Aunt Julie' from **Rings on a Tree** by Norman MacCaig. Alan Holden for 'The Circle' from **The Country Over** by Molly Holden, Chatto & Windus (1975). Geoffrey Holloway for 'The Balloon', 'Silver Birch', 'Dawn Chorus', 'Gale End' and 'Sweet Peas'. Maggie Holmes for 'For the First Time'. Hutchinson Publishing Group Ltd for part of 'Schoolmaster' by Yevgeny Yevtushenko and 'My Father's Hands' by Jeni Couzyn from **Say it Aloud** ed N Hidden (1972). Libby Houston for 'Talk about caves'. Jenny Joseph for 'Warning' from **Rose in the Afternoon**, J M Dent & Sons (1974). Jean Kenwood for 'Dragonfly'. John Lees for 'Floating Stuff'. London Management for 'How to Paint the Portrait of a Bird' by Jacques Prévert, translated by Paul Dehn from **My Kind of Verse**. Frances Lovell for 'Sunset'. Gerda Mayer for 'The Lodger'. John Moat for 'Three Promises' and 'Wendy's Song'. Peter Mortimer for 'Bald Bertie'. Madeline Munro for 'Cups' from **The Chant**, Yorick Books (1983). John Murray Ltd for 'Diary of a Church Mouse' from **Collected Poems** by John Betjeman (1958). Judith Nicholls for 'Lines' and 'Sea Dream'. Leslie Norris for 'Boy Flying' from **Over the Bridge**, Puffin (1981). William Oxley for 'The Unicorn and Lions' and 'Feline Metamorphosis'. Penguin Books Ltd for 'Song of the Whale', 'Hugger Mugger' and 'Useful Person' from **Hot Dog and Other Poems** by Kit Wright, Kestrel Books (1981) and 'A Boy's Head' from **Selected Poems** by Miroslav Holub translated by I Milner and G Theiner (1967). Laurence Pollinger Ltd on behalf of the Estate of Mrs Frieda Lawrence Ravagli for 'Things Men have Made' from **The Complete Poems of D H Lawrence**, and on behalf of William Carlos Williams for 'Blueflags' and 'The Motor Barge' from **Selected Poems** ed Charles Tomlinson, Penguin (1976) and 'The Ship Moves'. Felix Redmill for 'Thames'. Michael Rosen for 'Sulk'. Maurice Rutherford for 'Child at Christmas' and 'Strikebound'. Lawrence Sail for 'Knowing at Easter' and 'Christmas Night'. Vernon Scannell for 'Apple Raid' from **All the Day Through** ed Wes Magee, Bell and Hyman (1982). Martin Secker & Warburg Ltd for '1939' from **Collected Poems** by Alan Brownjohn. Howard Sergeant for 'A Finnish Legend'. Eric Slayter for 'Echo'. Nick Stimson for 'Sundays' from **In Magnet Air**, Phoenix Springwood (1980). Virago Press for 'There is an Old Man' from **Me Again** by Stevie Smith (1981) Copyright © James MacGibbon (1981). Margaret Toms for 'Hippo' and 'Rhinoceros'. Mrs A M Walsh for 'Extinction of the 21st Century Dodo' by John Walsh and 'Ann's Flowers' from **The Roundabout by the Sea** by John Walsh, Oxford University Press. Simon Williams for 'The Whales Sing' from **A Weight of Small Things**, Lincolnshire and Humberside Arts (1981).

Every effort has been made to trace all the copyright holders but if any have been inadvertently overlooked the publishers will be pleased to make the necessary arrangements at the first opportunity.

Illustrations by:

Sandra Avison pp16, 17, 46, 47, 78, 79, 80, 81   Amanda Carden pp 30, 31, 50, 51, 106, 107   Denise Carter pp 40, 41, 48, 49, 68, 69, 92, 93, 124, 125   Martin Farrar pp 24, 25, 36, 37, 54, 55, 86, 87, 104, 105   Barbara Glebska pp 32, 33, 44, 45, 76, 77, 102, 103   Anne Gowland pp 11, 12, 13, 28, 29, 60, 61, 62, 63   Thomas Keenes pp 10, 52, 53, 72, 73, 100, 101, 112, 113   Amanda Li pp 38, 39, 96, 97, 118, 119   John Loader pp 20, 21, 84, 85   Karen Lucas pp 58, 59, 94, 95, 110, 111   Mark Mason pp 8, 9, 70, 71, 82, 83, 88, 89   James Mayhew pp 14, 15, 22, 23, 90, 91, 108, 109   Eleni Michael pp 18, 19, 42, 43, 66, 67, 120, 121   James Peet pp 56, 57, 98, 99, 122, 123   Kevin Smith pp 26, 27, 64, 65, 116, 117   Anne Wilson pp 34, 35, 74, 75, 114, 115.

CONTENTS

The Unicorn and Lions

I met a unicorn in Trafalgar Square
That had been to visit the lions there,
With body white and a golden horn
It could never nuzzle and scarcely yawn.

'Where are you from?' I asked in surprise
But it shook its head and closed its eyes
And there it stood like a statue frozen
Under the column that was built for Nelson.

As can be imagined I was somewhat put out
Like many another who stopped thereabout;
But not for long were we left in the lurch
For there came a young girl through Admiralty Arch

A creature of innocence and obviously high-born
Anxiously seeking that lost unicorn.
Gently she called and immediately it went
And meek as a lamb allowed her to mount,

And away they went through pigeons and traffic
Along the Mall towards Buckingham Palace.
But not to be outdone I started to run
After the girl on the white unicorn.

Yet had not got far when I met an old fellow
Whose beard was white and whose face was yellow,
And he seized my arm and held it fast
Thus preventing me from going on past.

'Don't bother chasing 'em, young 'un' he said
'She's taking the unicorn back to its flag –
And no one'll see it again out walking
Afore the day there's another royal wedding.'

Then he let go my arm and away he shuffled
Leaving me alone but no longer baffled
By a unicorn met in Trafalgar Square
That had been to visit the lions there.

William Oxley

In the Picture

In the painting was a great crowd of people
and they all had flat faces:
pale, soft, waiting for expressions.

I wanted to fill in the blanks with a crayon:
curved lines for mouths smiling,
or scowls, or eyebrows lifted in surprise.

Then one of the figures moved a little:
an old woman near the front
dressed in brown, with a brown shawl.

She gestured with her hand, asked me to follow her
and I saw her face was not empty
but complete: she knew I would come.

Some of the others turned as I passed them
and I saw their faces were like hers;
but most stayed quite still, not watching.

She took me to see the thing that they had seen:
I saw it. Then I went back
out of the picture, the way I had come.

And I saw my face, mirrored in the picture glass:
it was soft, pale. I wanted a crayon
to draw myself a smile, or the lift of surprise.

Tony Charles

Useful Person

We'd missed the train. Two hours to wait
On Lime Street Station, Liverpool,
With *not a single thing to do*.
The bar was shut and Dad was blue
And Mum was getting in a state
And everybody felt a fool.

Yes, we were very glum indeed.
Myself, I'd nothing new to read,
No sweets to eat, no game to play.
'I'm bored,' I said, and straight away,
Mum said what I knew she'd say:
'Go on, then, read a book, O.K.?'
'I've *read* them *both*!' 'That's no excuse.'

Dad sat sighing, '*What* a day . . .
This is precious little use.
I wish they'd open up that bar.'
They didn't, though. No way.

And everybody else was sitting
In that waiting-room and knitting,
Staring, scratching, yawning, smoking.
'All right, Dad?' 'You must be joking!
This is precious little use.
It's like a prison. Turn me loose!'

('Big fool, act your age!' Mum hisses.
'Sorry, missus.'
'Worse than him, you are,' said Mum.)
And then the Mongol child came up,
Funny-faced:
Something in her body wrong,
Something in her mind
Misplaced:
Something in her eyes was strange:

What, or why, I couldn't tell:
But somehow she was beautiful
As well.

Anyway, she took us over!
'Hello, love,' said Dad. She said,
'*There*, sit *there*!' and punched a spot
On the seat. The spot was what,
Almost, Mum was sitting on,
So Dad squeezed up, and head-to-head,
And crushed-up, hip-to-hip, they sat.
'What next, then?' 'Kiss!' 'Oh no, not that!'
Dad said, chuckling. '*Kiss!*'

                  They did!

I thought my Mum would flip her lid
With laughing. Then the Mongol child
Was filled with pleasure – she went wild,
Running round the tables, telling
Everyone to *kiss* and yelling
Out to everyone to sit
Where she said. They did, too. It

Was sudden happiness because
The Mongol child
Was what she was:
Bossy, happy, full of fun,
And just *determined* everyone
Should have a good time too! We knew
That's what we'd got to do.

Goodness me, she took us over!
All the passengers for Dover,
Wolverhampton, London, Crewe –
Everyone from everywhere
Began to share
Her point of view! The more they squeezed,

And laughed, and fooled about, the more
The Mongol child
Was pleased!

Dad had to kiss another Dad
('Watch it, lad!' '*You* watch it, lad!'
'Stop: you're not my kind of bloke!')
Laugh? I thought that Mum would choke!

And so the time whirled by. The train
Whizzed us home again
And on the way I thought of her:
Precious little use is what
Things had been. Then she came
And things were not
The same!

She was precious, she was little,
She was useful too:
Made us speak when we were dumb,
Made us smile when we were blue,
Cheered us up when we were glum,
Lifted us when we were flat:
Who could be
More use than that?

Mongol child,
Funny-faced,
Something in your body wrong,
Something in your mind
Misplaced,
Something in your eyes, strange:
What, or why, I cannot tell:
I thought you were beautiful:

Useful, as well.

Kit Wright

Figure and Ground

It was after
Whatever happened –
Whatever happened?
I can't remember.
But it was after,
And I was walking
Along a street I think that once I must have known.
I was alone.
But then he came towards me,
A young boy,
Intent upon the bouncing of a ball.
Nearer he came, and nearer,
Bounce and skip,
And then he passed right through me
And I turned,
And watched him bouncing, skipping up the road
And did not know
I was the ghost, the ghost who passed through him,
But thought
He was the ghost, a ghost who passed through me.
And I was most afraid.

Pam Gidney

A Boy's Head

In it there is a space-ship
and a project
for doing away with piano lessons.

And there is
Noah's ark
which shall be first.

And there is
an entirely new bird,
an entirely new hare,
an entirely new bumble-bee.

There is a river
that flows upwards.

There is a multiplication table.
There is anti-matter.
And it just cannot be trimmed.

I believe
that only what cannot be trimmed
is a boy's head.

There is much promise
in the circumstances
that so many people have heads.

Miroslav Holub

Boy Flying

Flying,
   He saw the earth flat as a plate,
   As if there were no hills, as if houses
   Were only roofs, as if the trees
   Were only the leaves that covered
   The treetops. He could see the shadows
   The clouds cast when they sailed over the fields,
   He could see the river like the silver track
   Left by a snail, and roads narrow as ribbons.

   He could not see Mickey French next door,
   In bed with a cold, nor his two sisters
   Playing 'Happy Families' as they watched
   The television. He could not see his kitten.

Flying,
   He felt the air as solid as water
   When he spread his fingers against it.
   He felt it cool against his face, he felt
   His hair whipped. He felt weightless
   As if he were hollow, he felt the sun
   Enormously bright and warm on his back,
   He felt his eyes watering. He felt
   The small, moist drops the clouds held.

   He could not feel the grass, he could not
   Feel the rough stones of the garden wall.
   He could not remember the harsh, dry bark
   Of the apple tree against his knees.

Flying,
  He could hear the wind hissing, the note
  Changed when he turned his head. He heard
  His own voice when he sang. Very faintly,
  He heard the school bus as it grumbled
  Past the church, he thought he could hear
  The voices of the people as they shouted
  In amazement when they saw him swoop and glide.

  He could not hear the birds sing, nor the chalk
  Squeak against the blackboard, nor the mower
  As it whirred along, nor the clock tick.
  He could not hear the bacon sizzle in the pan,
  He could not hear his friend calling him.

Leslie Norris

Floating Stuff

One kick and I'm afloat,
walking on nothing, buoyed up
by my churning feet. My hair
ruffles the ceiling,
and I'm pumping away
on my invisible unicycle,
high above the others.

Only I can do this,
and then, only some nights,
blanket-deep in the old dream,
nudging the high ceiling of sleep.

The others can play their dull games
on the flat ground
where I'm always too slow,
too fat to catch them
and always *it* first

because up here, kick-flying,
I tread the air easily, floating
high in the special pigeon-holes
of my head.

John Lees

The Balloon

When I was six (and naughty)
God came to call;
stood at the lane end, in the air,
not moving, simply there.

Radish-red, angry,
taller than I'd ever thought,
taller than our cherry tree –
and broad, against that cobalt sky.

He looked as if he'd never move –
still, like me. But he did
– slow as a jellyfish –
down, down towards me

then went up, straight over,
showing his black mouth, beneath;
pulling my eyes out wide with him,
bigger, the smaller he went.

'Humph. Humph' was what he said
– gargling, snorting fire –
'Humph. Humph' over the tiny houses,
the quiet hill.

Geoffrey Holloway

1939

Where the ball ran into the bushes,
And I was sent to find it, being
Useful for that more than to play their game,
I saw instead
This badge, from someone's brother, in
Some regiment of that war: a trophy
Begged for and polished, coveted certainly,
But lost now, slightly touched with dust already,
Yet shining still, under smooth leaves drab with dust.
I knew that people prized such trophies then,
It was the way of all of us. I might,
For no one looked, have taken it
For mine. I valued it. It shone
For me as much as anyone.
And yet some fear or honesty, some sense
It wasn't to be mine – it wasn't more –
Said No to all of this. Besides,
They shouted in the distance for their ball.
For once quite quickly, I
Made up my mind
And left the thing behind.

Alan Brownjohn

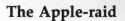

The Apple-raid

Darkness came early, though not yet cold;
Stars were strung on the telegraph wires;
Street lamps spilled pools of liquid gold;
The breeze was spiced with garden fires.

That smell of burnt leaves, the early dark,
Can still excite me but not as it did
So long ago when we met in the Park –
Myself, John Peters and David Kidd.

We moved out of town to the district where
The lucky and wealthy had their homes
With garages, gardens, and apples to spare
Ripely clustered in the trees' green domes.

We chose the place we meant to plunder
And climbed the wall and dropped down to
The secret dark. Apples crunched under
Our feet as we moved through the grass and dew.

The clusters on the lower boughs of the tree
Were easy to reach. We stored the fruit
In pockets and jerseys until all three
Boys were heavy with their tasty loot.

Safe on the other side of the wall
We moved back to town and munched as we went.
I wonder if David remembers at all
That little adventure, the apples' fresh scent?

Strange to think that he's fifty years old,
That tough little boy with scabs on his knees;
Stranger to think that John Peters lies cold
In an orchard in France beneath apple trees.

Vernon Scannell

In watchful community

In watchful community
when we ought to be at school

sheltering by the warehouse
we stand, smelling
creosote, and the musty
rot of wood from floorboards
where sacks have lain, for
years, huddled together.

That is behind us, but
in front we hear the
plop of rain, and
while we stand
our bodies are increasing
in secret society.

Thom Gunn

The Play Way

Sunlight pillars through glass, probes each desk
For milk-tops, drinking straws and old dry crusts.
The music strides to challenge it
Mixing memory and desire with chalk dust.

My lesson notes read: Teacher will play
Beethoven's Concerto Number Five
And class will express themselves freely
In writing. One said 'Can we jive?'

When I produced the record, but now
The big sound has silenced them. Higher
And firmer, each authoritative note
Pumps the classroom up tight as a tyre

Working its private spell behind eyes
That stare wide. They have forgotten me
For once. The pens are busy, the tongues mime
Their blundering embrace of the free

Word. A silence charged with sweetness
Breaks short on lost faces where I see
New looks. Then notes stretch taut as snares. They trip
To fall into themselves unknowingly.

Seamus Heaney

Schoolmaster

The window gives onto the white trees.
The master looks out of it at the trees,
for a long time, he looks for a long time
out through the window at the trees,
breaking his chalk slowly in one hand.
And it's only the rules of long division.
And he's forgotten the rules of long division.
Imagine not remembering long division!
A mistake on the blackboard, a mistake.
We watch him with a different attention
needing no one to hint to us about it,
there's more than difference in this attention.
The schoolmaster's wife has gone away,
we do not know where she has gone to,
we do not know why she has gone,
what we know is his wife has gone away.

His clothes are neither new nor in the fashion;
wearing the suit which he always wears
and which is neither new nor in the fashion
the master goes downstairs to the cloakroom.
We hear the door below creaking behind him.
The window gives onto the white trees.
The trees there are high and wonderful,
but they are not why we are looking out.

We look in silence at the schoolmaster.
He has a bent back and clumsy walk,
he moves without defences, clumsily,
worn out I ought to have said, clumsily.
Snow falling on him softly through silence
turns him to white under the white trees.
He whitens into white like the trees.
A little longer will make him so white
we shall not see him in the whitened trees.

Part of a poem by *Yevgeny Yevtushenko*,
translated by Peter Levi, S. J. & R Milner Gulland

Schoolmistress (Miss Humm)

Straight-backed as a Windsor chair
She stood on the top playground step
And surveyed her Saturnalian kingdom.
At 8.45 precisely, she stiffened
(If that were possible), produced a key
– A large, cold dungeon-key –
Placed it below her lip, and blew.

No summons from Heaven itself
(It was a church school) was more imperious!
No angel trumpet or Mosean thunder-clap
Calling the Israelites to doom or repentance
Met swifter obedience. No Gorgon
Suspended life with such efficiency.
In the middle of a shout, a scream,
We halted. Our faces froze.
No longer George or Tom or Mary,
But forty reproductions of a single child,
Chilled to conformity. We gathered
Like captive troops and, climbing steps,
Received the inspection of her cool eyes,
Willing them away from unwashed necks
Or black-ringed fingernails,
But knowing our very thoughts were visible
If she chose to see. Nothing escaped her.

She was (as I said, a church school)
God, St Michael, the Recording Angel
And, in our guiltier moments, Lucifer –
A Lucifer in long tweed skirts
And a blouse severely fastened at the neck
By a round cameo that was no ornament
But the outward sign of inward authority.
Even the Rector, when he stepped inside
And the brown walls rumbled to his voice,
Dwindled to a curate . . .
It would have astonished us to learn, I think,
That she ate supper, went to bed,
And even, perhaps, on occasions, slept.

Clive Sansom

The Astigmatic

At seven the sun that lit my world blew out
Leaving me only mist. Through which I probed
My way to school, guessed wildly at the sums
Whose marks on the board I couldn't even see.

They wanted to send me away to a special school.
I refused, and coped as best I could with half
The light lost in the mist, screwing my tears
Into my work, my gritted teeth, my writing –

Which crawled along and writhed. Think thoughts at will,
None of it comes across. Even now friends ask
'How do you read that scrawl?' The fact is, I don't;
Nobody could. I guess. But how would you

Like my world where parallels actually join,
Perspectives vary at sight? Once in a pub
I walked towards a sign marked gents over
A grating and crashed through the floor –

Well, it looked all right to me. Those steep stairs
People told me of later flattened to lines
In my half-world. The rest imagination
Supplied: when you've half a line you extend it.

The lenses drag their framework down my nose.
I still can't look strangers in the face,
Wilting behind a wall of glass at them.
It makes me look shifty at interviews.

I wake up with a headache, chew all day
Aspirins, go to bed dispirited,
Still with a dull pain somewhere in my skull,
And sleep. Then, in my dreams, the sun comes out.

Philip Hobsbaum

Lines

I must never daydream in schooltime.
I just love a daydream in Mayshine.
I must ever greydream in timeschool.
Why must others paydream in schoolway?
Just over highschool dismay lay.
Thrust over skydreams in cryschool.
Cry dust over drydreams in screamtime.
Dreamschool thirst first in dismayday.
Why lie for greyday in crimedream?
My time for dreamday is soontime.
In soontime must I daydream ever.
Never must I say dream in strifetime.
Cry dust over daydreams of lifetimes.
I must never daydream in schooltime.
In time I must daydream never.

Judith Nicholls

Teatime at our House

Everything daydreams at our house
except me.

The teapot thinks it's a goldfish.
Have you tried pouring tea from a goldfish?

The table thinks it's a turtle.
You can't have your tea off a turtle.

The washing machine thinks it's a camera.
You should try washing socks in a camera.

The soup bowl thinks it's a watch.
Have you tried eating soup from a watch?

Everything daydreams in our house
except me.
I'm happy being a Christmas tree.

George Inkerman

Where it is always Summer

Inside my head, behind my eyes
it is always summer.

A silver aeroplane sticks its nose
into the orange clouds, the sun

bursts a yellow balloon above
our house, but I could lie here

on any day beside the fire,
sew the rainclouds tightly up

and hurl them across the sea
so that they sink like stones

beneath the keels of pirate ships
that plunder the seven oceans.

The island is shaped like a skull,
deep in its heart
treasure is buried, hidden in caves.

Yellow doubloons tumble and spill
out of their sacks like grain.

I run my hands through the rich crop,
plough my fingers into the pile

and race to the seaplane riding
the salt-blue waves.

Coins crammed into my pockets
blaze as brightly as the sun.

My dreams grow in its golden fields
somewhere behind my eyes.

David Harmer

A Direct Road

In the first week of the autumn term
other children told
of Costa Brava, Costa del sol,
French Riviera and the Pyrenees.
I was silent. The shame of poverty
meant holidays were spent at home.

'Write about your holiday'. The dreaded
moment came each year. But once
my teacher gave a choice: 'or draw
the nicest of the places you have seen'.

Across the page I let the colours sprawl –
the purple ground of heather,
the golden splash of gorse.
Stumps of monumental trees
like broken pillars rose between
the humps and hillocks
of my summer hideaway.

I could not paint the music of the wind
that playing a backing to the humming grass,
nor show the richness of its earthy scent
fertile with spore and seed.

So on the dark horizon I sketched in
the mirage that it brought:
the towering cliffs of cloudland,
castles sparkling on the air like birds,
and through the crowded streets and park
shadows of men like trees
were dancing as they walked.

The teacher pinned my picture to the board
and praised my eye for detail.
'Where did you find this place?'
the envious children asked. I smiled:
'Just somewhere on the road,' I told them
but did not add
'between the gasworks and the station yard'.

Edna Eglinton

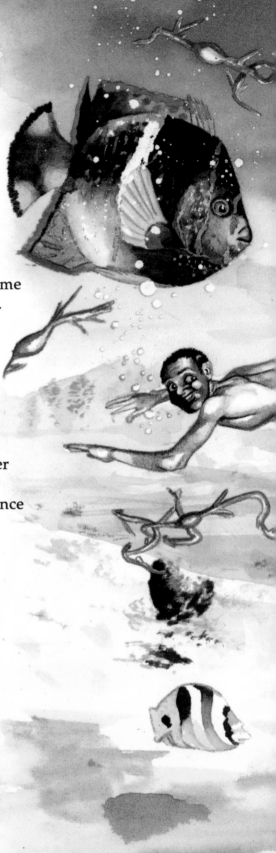

For the First Time

For the first time today
I opened my eyes
and saw

a whole new world
a silent translucent expanse
of jagged tiled white
a luminous encounter
of blue and green
where blurred figures
glided without sound about me
as I held my bubbled breath.

For the first time today
I opened my eyes and
saw – under water.

For the first time today
I trusted
Starfished on that same water
I had just explored
supported by water which once
I had feared so passionately
I drifted
human flotsam
mind and body lost
in watery equilibrium.

For the first time today
I floated –
and trusted an
alien element.

Maggie Holmes

Talk about caves

Talk about caves!
Tell us about them!
What's a cave, what's it like?

'My strongroom, mine,' said the Dragon,
'where I hid my gorgeous gold!'
But he lay gloating there so long
in the end, he turned to stone –
crawl down his twisting throat, you can,
for his breath's quite cold.

'My house once,'
whispered the Caveman's ghost.
'O it was good
wrapped in fur by the fire to hear
the roaring beasts in the wood
and sleep sound in earth's arms!
If you find my old knife there,
you can keep it.'

'My bolthole from the beginning,'
Night said,
'where I've stayed
safe from my enemy, Day.
I watch through a crack the sun
beating away at the door –
"Open up!" he shouts.
He'll never get in!'

'My home, always,' said Water.
'I wash my hands here
and slow as I like I make
new beds to lie on
in secret rooms
with pillows and curtains
and lovely ornaments,
pillars and plumes,
statues and thrones –
what colours the dark hides!
I shape earth's bones.'

'Don't disturb me,' the Bat said.
'This is where I hang my weary head.'

Libby Houston

Spoilsport

It's not that
I'm a scaredy cat,
it's just that
I don't like caves,
and the feeling of doom
in the colourless gloom
flowing over you
in waves.

It's the way
your voice rolls
round and around,
echoing low and weird,
and your torch becomes
such a little light,
each shadow one
to be feared.

It's the way
the clammy cold
grips you, chills you
through to your very bones,
and how every sound
when you're underground
is some unspeakable thing
that groans.

It's the way
that you slip
on slime underfoot and it's
hard to remember the sun,
so when kids want to explore
all the caves on the shore
I say, 'Count *me* out.
It's no fun!'

Moira Andrew

Sea Dream

I wander the deep-sea forests
where the snake-fish slither;
where the dark dunes drift
like rolling mist
and the white whales murmur.

I wake to coral blossom
and sleep in a star-clad cave;
my bed is a glade
of ribboned jade,
my sky a wave.

I dance by the spiny urchin
and ride the giant clam;
I feel as I sail
the dolphin's tail
the sad whale song.

Judith Nicholls

The whales sing

The whales sing
in songs of sonar;
sad ballads
of two hundred years
echo with the current.

They sing of
heroes in the north
whose breath
showered a hundred feet,
whose tails made the seas move,

of battles
where harpoons cracked,
of jaws
that pulled their boats apart,
of deaths they could not count.

The whales sing
in hope of their return.
Their choirs
of many hollow voices
grow more lonely.

They sing with
a stream of consciousness
dissolving
like impurities
in their frozen, chainsawed flesh.

Simon Williams

The Song of the Whale

Heaving mountain in the sea,
Whale, I heard you
Grieving.

Great whale, crying for your life,
Crying for your kind, I knew
How we would use
Your dying:

Lipstick for our painted faces,
Polish for our shoes.

Tumbling mountain in the sea,
Whale, I heard you
Calling.

Bird-high notes, keening, soaring:
At their edge a tiny drum
Like a heartbeat.

We would make you
Dumb.

In the forest of the sea,
Whale, I heard you
Singing,

Singing to your kind.
We'll never let you be.
Instead of life we choose

Lipstick for our painted faces,
Polish for our shoes.

Kit Wright

Extinction of the 21st Century Dodo

(For the Dodo think Whale, Fox, Badger etc)

The Dodo said
to the kangaroo
I wish I could jump
and skip away like you

The Dodo said
to the goat and the ape
I wish I could climb
so I can escape

The Dodo said
to the birds in the trees
I wish I could fly
and float in the breeze

The Dodo said
to the fish in the sea
I wish I could swim
so I could be free

The Dodo said
to the ant and the mole
I wish I was small
so I could hide in a hole

The Dodo said
to the man with a gun
why do you kill me
just for fun?

The Dodo said
to God in Heaven
why'd you let man
invent that weapon?

J. Walsh

Barbara Glebska

Shut your Eyes or Turn your Head

The cages have gone
Even the high mesh
Of the bird cage
Has disappeared.
Along with the penguins
And monkey and snakes
Went the jaguar, lion,
Leopard and elephant.
They all went together
At the same instant
That I shut my eyes.

If I shut my eyes
The words have gone
From the page,
So has the wall and door.
You too have gone.

Then I open my eyes
And in the zoo all round
I see folk in houses
In cars on television
On streets and in schools,
Everywhere I look
I can see people
Even in the cracks of the ceiling
Or outlined in clouds
Or beneath water,
In fire blaze.
And in this zoo
I see creatures caged.

Poor jaguar I would rather
Shut my eyes forever
Than see you forever caged.
But I must open them
Or I will bump into
What I cannot see.
Which proves perhaps
That I don't see everything
Even with eyes wide open.

I might bark my shins
On something obvious to you
Which I cannot see
Because I was looking
At something else.

There are many things
I'd rather not see I know
Some of them like the lion and jaguar
In the cage and people so jumbled
Together that they roll
Into a huge ball all arms and fingers
Clutching at something
That is never there.
I close my eyes to that.

John Fairfax

Rhinoceros

The rhino's thick and rigid hide
has baggy bits, to move inside;
and on his weighted head is worn
an edifice of chunky horn
said to be stiff with potent magic
(a superstition far from truth).
In view of this belief, it's tragic
his armour isn't bullet-proof.

Margaret Toms

Hippo

The hippo is a visual joke,
inflated like a rubber bed,
whose little bulging features poke
out of a yawning head.

Her jaws are built to match her girth,
with palate ribbed for emphasis.
Full-fed, she flops upon the earth
and smiles with rosy bliss.

But when she launches from the verge
to swim with curved aquatic grace,
those nostrils, eyes and ears emerge
above a hidden face –

and as by underwater bulk
you're comprehensively surveyed . . .
is hippo an ungainly hulk?
Or marvellously made?

Margaret Toms

giraffe

an
almost
ridiculously
triangular head
at
the
sha
key
top
ofa
lon
gth
inn
eck
giraffes are made of dirty yel
low plasticene and four

m	s
a	t
t	i
c	c
h	k
	s

dave calder

ELEPHANT

is very huge is
ELEPHANT
and Big and Bulky
and everso even
PonDerOus;
and he thinks he thinks
but he doesn't know what
he thinks he thinks:
are very huge are
ELEPHANT THOUGHTS
and Weighty and Large
and very hard
but soft underneath,
and he thinks he thinks
its time for hay
but he doesn't know
and that being so
he squirts water over
his big left shoulder
and thinks of a very huge
NOTHING.

is very huge is
ELEPHANT
Is hugely ENORMOUS
(and also slightly gormless)

dave calder

Camel

'I confess,' said the camel, 'I sometimes wish
My hump wasn't shaped like a pudding-dish.
We might have been fitted with something pretty –
Like the Turkish mosque at the old white city;
Or why not a statue or a flower,
Or a helmet and crest or a tree, or a tower
Carved with scenes from some classical story, all
In marble and gold, like the Albert Memorial?'

'Well, well,' I said mildly, 'there's no deciding –
But a tree'd be rather a nuisance when riding.'

Christopher Isherwood

Ostrich

Large cold farms in sandy places
– to be an ostrich is serious and difficult.

An eagle has a dignity already, an ostrich
has to try to make his own.

Ostriches have to learn to be thought stupid
and not mind it,
have to learn to stand about in gawky, plumed
   groups
and be laughed at by a lot of foolish people
as a lot of foolish birds
and not resent it.

Little ostriches
fumble out of their big eggs to be told,
'Patience is the thing, dear, an impatient
   ostrich
is making trouble for himself.'

An ostrich's life is a hard life which you
   sometimes
feel you could run away from.
Sometimes you even think it just won't
bear looking at any more.

But in the end it's a worthwhile
   job with good prospects and if you
      still want to apply to be an ostrich
         send for the forms today.

Alan Brownjohn

My mother saw a dancing bear

My mother saw a dancing bear
By the schoolyard, a day in June.
The keeper stood with chain and bar
And whistle-pipe, and played a tune.

And bruin lifted up its head
And lifted up its dusty feet,
And all the children laughed to see
It caper in the summer heat.

They watched as for the Queen it died.
They watched it march. They watched it halt.
They heard the keeper as he cried,
'Now, roly-poly!' 'Somersault!'

And then, my mother said, there came
The keeper with a begging-cup,
The bear with burning coat of fur,
Shaming the laughter to a stop.

They paid a penny for the dance,
But what they saw was not the show;
Only, in bruin's aching eyes,
Far-distant forests, and the snow.

Charles Causley

Galactic cat

Galactic cat
Prowling between the planets
Pussyfooting along paths
Untrodden hitherto
By feline feet,
Searches the Milky Way
But finds no sustenance there.

Back arched,
Galactic Puss
Passes the Dog Star,
Claws unsheathed;
Silently pads
Back to his home
Somewhere beyond Epsilon Aurigae,
There turns and turns
In soft self-orbit
Following his tail,
Then settles down
To warm his fur
Before the galaxies'
Cold fire.

Pam Gidney

Feline Metamorphosis

Our cat who's fat
and black as a bush
with snow on it
spends all day thinking
about filling his belly:
it's disgraceful really,
disgusting,
the way he's becoming
quite human.

William Oxley

Cat-Poem

I let you walk all over me,
wet feet and all, before you lie
uncomfortably across my lap.

Soon you are stretched belly upward,
mouth a useful leather purse,
paws limp with mice you've let go.

Or you cling like a cravat
to my chest, and I patch
my days with your black shape.

I try to figure you out, prise
you with words, but you are not
domesticable, and remain beyond call.

Joan Downar

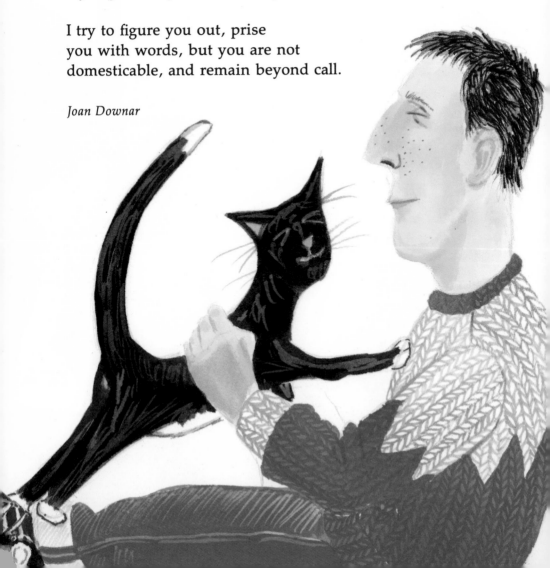

Requiem

The spider wove out across the room.
Four pairs of co-ordinated rapid legs
Silently bore along his blob of a body
An inch above the carpet.

A dropped boll of cottonwool
Halted him in mid-rush.
He poised to assess the danger,
Reassured, rushed on.

The ginger cat
Raised an eyebrow, pricked an ear.
Attentively she watched his darting course,
And as he coasted near, with casual accuracy
Bent her head and gathered up
The spider. Her mouth
For a moment was fringed
With brown brittle legs until
She swallowed down
The little bit of protein.

Pamela Gillilan

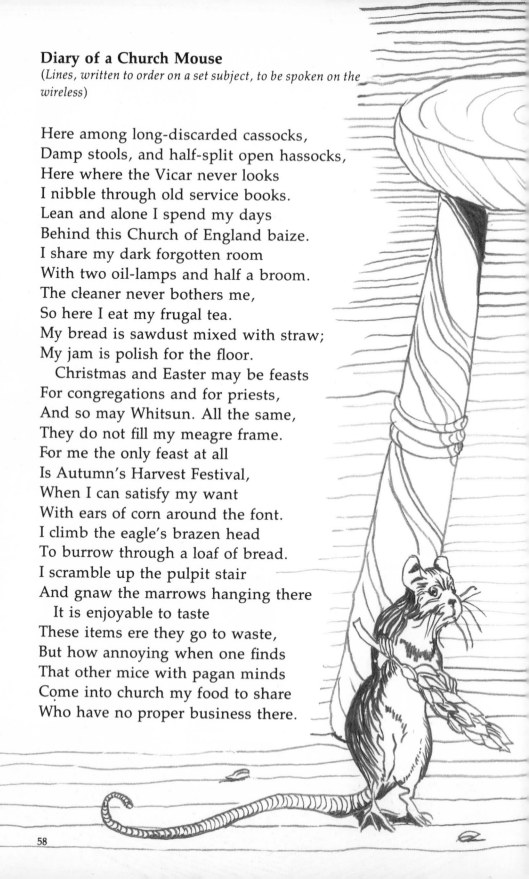

Diary of a Church Mouse

(Lines, written to order on a set subject, to be spoken on the wireless)

Here among long-discarded cassocks,
Damp stools, and half-split open hassocks,
Here where the Vicar never looks
I nibble through old service books.
Lean and alone I spend my days
Behind this Church of England baize.
I share my dark forgotten room
With two oil-lamps and half a broom.
The cleaner never bothers me,
So here I eat my frugal tea.
My bread is sawdust mixed with straw;
My jam is polish for the floor.
    Christmas and Easter may be feasts
For congregations and for priests,
And so may Whitsun. All the same,
They do not fill my meagre frame.
For me the only feast at all
Is Autumn's Harvest Festival,
When I can satisfy my want
With ears of corn around the font.
I climb the eagle's brazen head
To burrow through a loaf of bread.
I scramble up the pulpit stair
And gnaw the marrows hanging there
    It is enjoyable to taste
These items ere they go to waste,
But how annoying when one finds
That other mice with pagan minds
Come into church my food to share
Who have no proper business there.

Two field mice who have no desire
To be baptized, invade the choir.
A large and most unfriendly rat
Comes in to see what we are at.
He says he thinks there is no God
And yet he comes . . . it's rather odd.
This year he stole a sheaf of wheat
(It screened our special preacher's seat),
And prosperous mice from fields away
Come in to hear the organ play,
And under cover of its notes
Ate through the altar's sheaf of oats.
A Low Church mouse, who thinks that I
Am too papistical, and High,
Yet somehow doesn't think it wrong
To munch through Harvest Evensong,
While I, who starve the whole year through,
Must share my food with rodents who
Except at this time of the year
Not once inside the church appear.

Within the human world I know
Such goings-on could not be so,
For human beings only do
What their religion tells them to.
They read the Bible every day
And always, night and morning, pray,
And just like me, the good church mouse,
Worship each week in God's own house,

But all the same it's strange to me
How very full the church can be
With people I don't see at all
Except at Harvest Festival.

John Betjeman

Singing Game

(The Round House, c. 1830, is built over a broken market cross at Newport, Launceston, Cornwall)

Here we go round the Round House
In the month of one,
Looking to the eastward
For the springing sun.
The sky is made of ashes,
The trees are made of bone,
And all the water in the well
Is stubborn as a stone.

Here we go round the Round House
In the month of two,
Waiting for the weather
To thaw my dancing shoe.
In St Thomas River
Hide the freckled trout,
But for dinner on Friday
I shall pull one out.

Here we go round the Round House
In the month of three,
Listening for the bumble
Of the humble-bee.
The light is growing longer,
The geese begin to lay,
The song-thrush in the church-yard
Charms the cold away.

Here we go round the Round House
In the month of four,
Watching a couple dressed in green
Dancing through the door.
One wears a wreath of myrtle,
Another, buds of thorn:
God grant that all men's children
Be as sweetly born.

Here we go round the Round House
In the month of five,
Waiting for the summer
To tell us we're alive.
All round the country
The warm seas flow,
The devil's on an ice-cap
Melting with the snow.

Here we go round the Round House
In the month of six;
High in the tower
The town clock ticks.
Hear the black quarter-jacks
Beat the noon bell;
They say the day is half away
And the year as well.

Here we go round the Round House
In the month of seven,
The river running thirsty
From Cornwall to Devon.
The sun is on the hedgerow,
The cattle in the stream,
And one will give us strawberries
And one will give us cream.

Here we go round the Round House
In the month of eight,
Hoping that for harvest
We shall never wait.
Slyly the sunshine
Butters up the bread
To bear us through the winter
When the light is dead.

Here we go round the Round House
In the month of nine,
Watching the orchard apple
Turning into wine.
The day after tomorrow
I'll take one from the tree
And pray the worm will do no harm
If it comes close to me.

Here we go round the Round House
In the month of ten,
While the cattle winter
In the farmer's pen.
Thick the leaves are lying
On the coppice floor;
Such a coat against the cold
Never a body wore.

Here we go round the Round House
In the month of eleven,
The sea-birds swiftly flying
To the coast of heaven.
The plough is in the furrow,
The boat is on the strand;
May I be fed on fish and bread
While water lies on land.

Here we go round the Round House
In the month of twelve,
The hedgers break the brier
And the ditchers delve.
As we go round the Round House
May the moon and sun
Guide us to tomorrow
And the month of one:
And life be never done.

Charles Causley

January

A sealed stillness
– only the stream moves,
tremor and furl of water
under dead leaves.

In silence
the wood declares itself:
angles and arabesques of darkness,
branch, bramble,
tussocks of ghost grass
– under my heel
ice shivers
frail blue as sky
between the runes of trees.

Far up
rooks, crows
flail home.

Frances Horovitz

Giant Winter

Giant Winter preys on the earth,
Gripping with talons of ice,
Squeezing, seeking a submission,
Tightening his grip like a vice.

Starved of sunlight shivering trees
Are bent by his torturing breath.
The seeds burrow into the soil
Preparing to fight to the death.

Giant Winter sneers at their struggles,
Blows blizzards from his frozen jaws,
Ripples cold muscles of iron,
Clenches tighter his icicle claws.

Just as he seems to be winning,
Strength suddenly ebbs from his veins.
He releases his hold and collapses.
Giant Spring gently takes up the reins.

Snarling, bitter with resentment,
Winter crawls to his polar den,
Where he watches and waits till it's time
To renew the battle again.

Derek Stuart

At Candlemas

'If Candlemas be fine and clear
There'll be two winters in that year';

But all the day the drumming sun
Brazened it out that spring had come,

And the tall elder on the scene
Unfolded the first leaves of green.

But when another morning came
With frost, as Candlemas with flame,

The sky was steel, there was no sun,
The elder leaves were dead and gone.

Out of a cold and crusted eye
The stiff pond stared up at the sky,

And on the scarcely-breathing earth
A killing wind fell from the north;

But still within the elder tree
The strong sap rose, though none could see.

Charles Causley

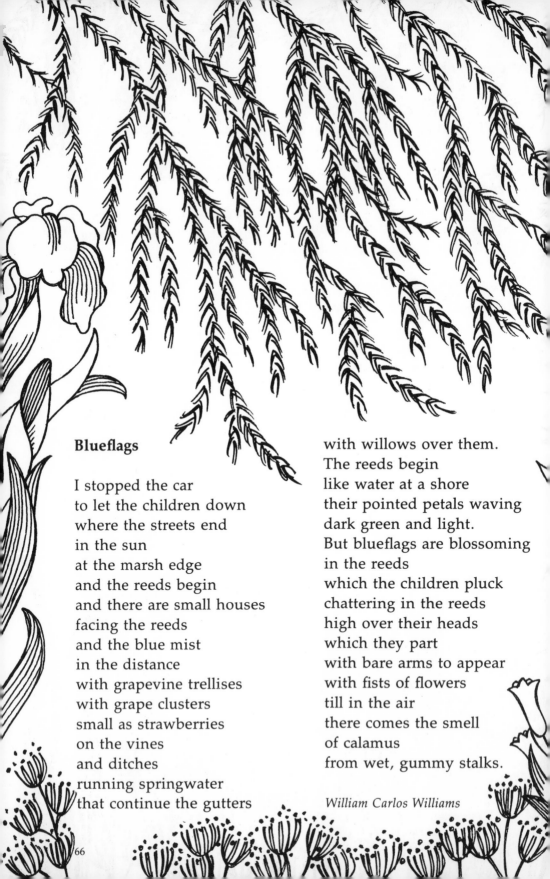

Blueflags

I stopped the car
to let the children down
where the streets end
in the sun
at the marsh edge
and the reeds begin
and there are small houses
facing the reeds
and the blue mist
in the distance
with grapevine trellises
with grape clusters
small as strawberries
on the vines
and ditches
running springwater
that continue the gutters

with willows over them.
The reeds begin
like water at a shore
their pointed petals waving
dark green and light.
But blueflags are blossoming
in the reeds
which the children pluck
chattering in the reeds
high over their heads
which they part
with bare arms to appear
with fists of flowers
till in the air
there comes the smell
of calamus
from wet, gummy stalks.

William Carlos Williams

Dragonfly

Over the pond
where the children play
I saw somebody
strange, today:
a slender, glittering,
trembling thing
with stuff like cellophane
on its wing.

It wasn't a butterfly
or bee
lolloping, blundering,
loose and free . . .
it darted here
and it darted there
like a quivering firework
in the air.

Down by the pond
I stared, and stood
in the heat of the morning.
I wished it would
stay and settle,
but it went by,
burning, beautiful –
dragonfly.

Jean Kenward

Adlestrop

Yes. I remember Adlestrop –
The name, because one afternoon
Of heat the express-train drew up there
Unwontedly. It was late June.

The steam hissed. Some one cleared his throat.
No one left and no one came
On the bare platform. What I saw
Was Adlestrop – only the name

And willows, willow-herb, and grass,
And meadowsweet, and haycocks dry,
No whit less still and lonely fair
Than the high cloudlets in the sky.

And for that minute a blackbird sang
Close by, and round him, mistier,
Farther and farther, all the birds
Of Oxfordshire and Gloucestershire.

Edward Thomas

Flowers

(for Winifred Nicholson)

     Flowers,
a dozen or more,
I picked one summer afternoon
from field and hedgerow.
Resting against a wall
I held them up
to hide the sun.
Cell by cell,
exact as dance,
I saw the colour,
structure, purpose
of each flower.
I named them with their secret names.
They flamed in air.

     But, waking
I remember only two
– soapwort and figwort,
the lilac and the brown.
The rest I guess at
but cannot see
– only myself,
almost a ghost upon the road,
without accoutrement,
holding the flowers
as torch and talisman
against the coming dark.

Frances Horovitz

69

Ann's Flowers

Ann with hot fingers grasped her flowers
   A long half-day
'See, they are withering, Ann; you'd best
   Thrown them away.'

Yet still through lane and by-way on
   And on she trailed,
Till scent of flowers was one with warmth
   Of hand that held.

But when she knew that water now
   Would never bring
Freshness, she found a bank, with moss
   For covering;

There, lulled by reeds of grass and cooled
   By shade of tree,
A bed she made, in which they could
   Die quietly.

John Walsh

Still Life

The day is deadlocked by heat.
Doors stand open all along
the street and telephones
are silent.
       A baby cries
in a thin half-hearted way
too hot to feed, too sweated
for sleep. Lawn mowers idle
in empty gardens; sprinklers
mizzle to themselves in great
pinwheels on the grass.
Washing hangs dead-crow limp
and flowers faint.
           I swing
slow circles of lettuce
in its wire basket, water
drizzling warm over bare feet.

Moira Andrew

There Came a Day

There came a day that caught the summer
Wrung its neck
Plucked it
And ate it.

Now what shall I do with the trees?
The day said, the day said.
Strip them bare, strip them bare.
Let's see what is really there.

And what shall I do with the sun?
The day said, the day said.
Roll him away till he's cold and small.
He'll come back rested if he comes back at all.

And what shall I do with the birds?
The day said, the day said.
The birds I've frightened, let them flit,
I'll hang out pork for the brave tomtit.

And what shall I do with the seed?
The day said, the day said.
Bury it deep, see what it's worth.
See if it can stand the earth.

What shall I do with the people?
The day said, the day said.
Stuff them with apple and blackberry pie –
They'll love me then till the day they die.

There came this day and he was autumn.
His mouth was wide
And red as a sunset.
His tail was an icicle.

Ted Hughes

Gale End

Abruptly as the wind came, it drops. Careened and skidded,
the moon's dhow across a gulf suddenly
blue repentant rights itself.

Oakleaves a minute since harpooned by hidden lightnings
settle; as if bronze struck
decorate a hill's lapel.

The wood, that hissing furnace, sighs into white geometry:
ashes, skeletons so fire-delicate
they seem to live the name.

And we sit, amazed survivors, in a calm nook, a weather's
    valley . . .
into vivid silence.

Geoffrey Holloway

Leaves

Who's killed the leaves?
Me, says the apple, I've killed them all.
Fat as a bomb or a cannonball
I've killed the leaves.

Who sees them drop?
Me, says the pear, they will leave me all bare
So all the people can point and stare.
I see them drop.

Who'll catch their blood?
Me, me, me, says the marrow, the marrow.
I'll get so rotund that they'll need a wheelbarrow.
I'll catch their blood.

Who'll make their shroud?
Me, says the swallow, there's just time enough
Before I must pack all my spools and be off.
I'll make their shroud.

Who'll dig their grave?
Me, says the river, with the power of the clouds
A brown deep grave I'll dig under my floods.
I'll dig their grave.

Who'll be their parson?
Me, says the Crow, for it is well-known
I study the bible right down to the bone.
I'll be their parson.

Who'll be chief mourner?
Me, says the wind, I will cry through the grass
The people will pale and go cold when I pass.
I'll be chief mourner.

Who'll carry the coffin?
Me, says the sunset, the whole world will weep
To see me lower it into the deep.
I'll carry the coffin.

Who'll sing a psalm?
Me, says the tractor, with my gear grinding glottle
I'll plough up the stubble and sing through my throttle.
I'll sing the psalm.

Who'll toll the bell?
Me, says the robin, my song in October
Will tell the still gardens the leaves are over.
I'll toll the bell.

Ted Hughes

Christmas Night

On the wind, a drifting echo
of simple songs. In the city
the streetlamps, haloed innocents,
click into instant sleep.
The darkness at last breathes.

In dreams of wholeness, irony
is a train melting to distance;
and the word, a delighted child
gazing in safety at
a star solid as flesh.

Lawrence Sail

Child at Christmas

He was happy with the manger,
hot breath of oxen, starfall of carols,
shepherds and simplicity.

Why did they spoil it
with red cloak of make-believe
trimmed with white lies,
bitterness of dawning truth
and loss of trust.
How long, for their sakes,
must he now pretend belief?

He didn't need the tinsel
and the trimmings.

Maurice Rutherford

Waiting

Waiting, waiting, waiting
  For the party to begin;
Waiting, waiting, waiting
  For the laughter and din;
Waiting, waiting, waiting
  With hair just so
And clothes trim and tidy
  From top-knot to toe.
The floor is all shiny,
  The lights are ablaze;
There are sweetmeats in plenty
  And cakes beyond praise.
Oh the games and dancing,
  The tricks and the toys,
The music and the madness
  The colour and noise!
Waiting, waiting, waiting
  For the first knock on the door –
Was ever such waiting,
  Such waiting before?

James Reeves

My Party

My parents said I could have a party
And that's just what I did.

Dad said, 'Who had you thought of inviting?'
I told him. He said, 'Well, you'd better start writing,'
And that's just what I did

To:

Phyllis Willis, Horace Morris,
Nancy, Clancy, Bert and Gert Sturt,
Dick and Mick and Nick Crick,
Ron, Don, John,
Dolly, Molly, Polly –
Neil Peel –
And my dear old friend, Dave Dirt.

I wrote, 'Come along, I'm having a party,'
And that's just what they did.

They all arrived with huge appetites
As Dad and I were fixing the lights.
I said, 'Help yourself to the drinks and the bites!'
And that's just what they did,
All of them:

Phyllis Willis, Horace Morris,
Nancy, Clancy, Bert and Gert Sturt,
Dick and Mick and Nick Crick,
Ron, Don, John,
Dolly, Molly, Polly –
Neil Peel –
And my dear old friend, Dave Dirt.

Now, I had a good time and as far as I could tell,
The party seemed to go pretty well –
Yes, that's just what it did.

Then Dad said, 'Come on, just for fun,
Let's have a *turn* from everyone!'
And a turn's just what they did,

All of them:

Phyllis Willis, Horace Morris,
Nancy, Clancy, Bert and Gert Sturt,
Dick and Mick and Nick Crick,
Ron, Don, John,
Dolly, Molly, Polly –
Neil Peel –
And my dear old friend, Dave Dirt.

AND THIS IS WHAT THEY DID:

Phyllis and Clancy
And Horace and Nancy
Did a song and dance number
That was really fancy –

Dolly, Molly, Polly,
Ron, Don, and John
Performed a play
That went on and on and on –

Gert and Bert Sturt,
Sister and brother,
Did an imitation of
Each other.

(Gert Sturt put on Bert Sturt's shirt
And Bert Sturt put on Gert Sturt's skirt.)

Neil Peel
All on his own
Danced an eightsome reel.

Dick and Mick
And Nicholas Crick
Did a most *ingenious*
Conjuring trick

And my dear old friend, Dave Dirt,
Was terribly sick
All over the flowers.
We cleaned it up.
It took *hours*.

But as Dad said, giving a party's not easy.
You really
Have to
Stick at it.
I agree. And if Dave gives a party
I'm certainly
Going to be
Sick at it.

Kit Wright

Party Conversation

The party was really a nice one,
Though, of course, the boys got a bit rough.
We had jelly and ice creams and migraines for tea,
I think we all had quite enough.

The fancy dress was quite funny,
Diedre came as a toilet roll,
At which Mummy said something awful,
Though it could have been, 'Bless my soul!'

It was Sally who won all the prizes,
She came as a shrymph full of tea.
I'm not sure that is quite right though,
But that's how it sounded to me.

Near the end Billy Jones tore my costume
In a place that I'd rather not tell.
Though later he tripped on the carpet
And mucked up his costume as well.

John Cotton

Sulk

I'm sulking.
No one's going to make me eat a tomato
I can't stand tomatoes.
You know
when you bite them
there's all that slimy stuff;
there are all those little lumpy bits
in the slimy stuff
and it all slides round your tongue
and it all slides round your teeth.

And the fleshy bits
give me the shudders.
I feel little shivers
down the back of my neck
when the tomato is in my mouth.

So I'm not eating that tomato.

'You eat what's on your plate, lad.'
'No.'
'Well, there's nothing else
till you've eaten it.'

'I don't want nothing else.'
'What – tomorrow? The day after that?'
'No.'

'We'll see about that, I can tell you.'

So
I'm
sulking.
I'm
not
going
to eat
the
tomato
and I'm going to stay in a sulk
till I get something else to eat
even if it takes me all week.
Shut my mouth,
push my lips out,
make my eyes go dead.
Sulk.

Michael Rosen

The Stolen Orange

When I went out I stole an orange
I kept it in my pocket
It felt like a warm planet

Everywhere I went smelt of oranges
Whenever I got into an awkward situation
I'd take the orange out and smell it

And immediately on even dead branches I saw
The lovely and fierce orange blossom
That smells so much of joy

When I went out I stole an orange
It was a safeguard against imagining
there was nothing bright or special in the world

Brian Patten

Neighbour

An old lady sits quietly against her cottage wall.
In the morning sun she rests at one
With her home.
Timber for line, mortar for crease,
She has put her hand on the brick and wood
All the building of her days
Until each part melts together this morning
In the spring sun –
While I restlessly gaze from my page
To focus through a window
And wandering eye.

John Fairfax

Sundays

Coming in from the sun
With the juice of fresh cut grass
Staining my shoes and hands

To an odour of roast meat
And used vegetable dishes
Mixed heavy in the air with dust

I sat, and stared through
Open french windows at my father
Caught in colour coaxing the soil

To the ordered pace of blossom.
He would stop in mid-afternoon
To take tea, and looking up

See me and smile.
Carved in the silent heat
Where only butterflies move.

Nick Stimson

This morning my father

This morning my father looks out the window, rubs
   his nose
and says: Lets go and saw up logs
me and you.
So I put on my thick blue socks
and he puts on his army vest
and he keeps saying: Are you ready are you ready
It's a snorter of a day just look at the trees
and I run downstairs to get my old bent boots
that everybody says go round corners on their own
   they're so bent
and he comes in saying that his tobacco is like old
   straw
which means that he is going to smoke his pipe today
So he says to mum: We'll be back in an hour or two
which means not for ages
but mum doesn't hear, because we lumberjacks are
   out the door in a flash

Michael Rosen

Uncle Tom

'I'll tell you what we'll do boy,
Get two ponies, camping gear and food,
And, travelling light, each night we'll camp
Where day's end finds us.
You'll like that, the camp fires and the woods.'
And there's no doubt I would have done.

Often we talked of it,
My Uncle and I. He fresh-faced,
With something of the countryman,
Though if he had ever been such
I'm not sure. He could certainly ride well,
Sit a horse, I'll say that.
Learnt as a trooper in the cavalry.

Often I dreamed of it:
Lush lazy days beside a pony,
Sleeping under stars, and the bright mornings
Wonderfully fresh, the freedom and the air;
But they never came.
And, as in time, I knew they never would,
I didn't hold it against him,

Those promises, the hopes he raised.
Even now, the boy near two score on,
Uncle long dead, I occasionally remember
And gain some pleasure from it.

John Cotton

Aunt Julia

Aunt Julia spoke Gaelic
very loud and very fast.
I could not answer her –
I could not understand her.

She wore men's boots
when she wore any.
– I can see her strong foot,
stained with peat,
paddling the treadle of the spinningwheel
while her right hand drew yarn
marvellously out of the air.

Hers was the only house
where I've lain at night
in the absolute darkness
of a box bed, listening to
crickets being friendly.

She was buckets
and water flouncing into them.
She was winds pouring wetly
round house-ends.
She was brown eggs, black skirts
and a keeper of threepenny bits
in a teapot.

Aunt Julia spoke Gaelic
very loud and very fast.
By the time I had learned
a little, she lay
silenced in the absolute black
of a sandy grave
at Luskentyre.

But I hear her still, welcoming me
with a seagull's voice
across a hundred yards
of peatscrapes and lazybeds
and getting angry, getting angry
with so many questions
unanswered.

Norman MacCaig

Hugger Mugger

I'd sooner be
Jumped and thumped and dumped,

I'd sooner be
Slugged and mugged . . . than *hugged* . . .

And clobbered with a slobbering
Kiss by my Auntie Jean:

You know what I mean:

Whenever she comes to stay,
You know you're bound
To get one.
A quick
    short
    peck
    would
    be
    O.K.
But this is a
Whacking great
Smacking great
Wet one!

All whoosh and spit
And crunch and squeeze
And '*Dear* little boy!'
And 'Auntie's missed you!'
And 'Come to Auntie, she
Hasn't *kissed* you!'
Please don't do it, Auntie,
PLEASE!

And nothing on *earth* can persuade you
Not to,

The trick
Is to make it
Quick,

You know what I mean?

For as things are,
I really would far,

Far sooner be
Jumped and thumped and dumped,

I'd sooner be
Slugged and mugged . . . than *hugged* . . .

And clobbered with a slobbering
Kiss by my Auntie

Jean!

Kit Wright

Bald Bertie

Bertie was bald, as bald as can be
Bald as a light-bulb, a freshly shelled pea
As he walked down the street, the kids yelled 'Mister!'
'How come yer bonce looks just like a blister?'

Chorus (Vivace)
Oh! Oh! Bertie!
And still not thirty!

He applied several lotions, he massaged in cream
He dolloped on potions – by the ton (was HE keen!)
In a trim-fit wig, revved his new sports coupee;
too fast with a girl, and off flew his toupee

Chorus
Oh! Oh! Bertie!
And still not thirty!

Spoke to doctors, answered adverts, (alas, none the wiser)
Sweated hours in a greenhouse, smeared his nut with fertiliser
Wrote as 'Anxious, Bognor Regis, seeking help from *'Dear
      Dianne'*
Thumped his hairy dog called Norman, grew quite desperate
      (like Dan).

Chorus
Oh! Oh! Bertie!
And still not thirty!

Until one day he vanished, with no forwarding address
Left one sock and well-worn toothbrush, a bed that was a mess
Some say that he's in heaven, or very soon will be.
But who's that lonely figure in the tight-fitting trilby?

Chorus
Oh! Oh! Bertie!
And still not thirty!

Peter Mortimer

Riley

Down in the water-meadows Riley
Spread his wash on the bramble-thorn,
Sat, one foot in the moving water,
Bare as the day that he was born.

Candid was his curling whisker,
Brown his body as an old tree-limb,
Blue his eye as the jay above him
Watching him watch the minjies swim.

Four stout sticks for walls had Riley,
His roof was a rusty piece of tin,
As snug in the lew of a Cornish hedgerow
He watched the seasons out and in.

He paid no rates, he paid no taxes,
His lamp was the moon hung in the tree.
Though many an ache and pain had Riley
He envied neither you nor me.

Many a friend from bush or burrow
To Riley's hand would run or fly,
And soft he'd sing and sweet he'd whistle
Whatever the weather in the sky.

Till one winter's morning Riley
From the meadow vanished clean.
Gone was the rusty tin, the timber,
As if old Riley had never been.

What strange secret had old Riley?
Where did he come from? Where did he go?
Why was his heart as light as summer?
Never know now, said the jay. *Never know.*

Charles Causley

minjies: small minnows
lew: lee

There is an old man

There is an old man
Who sleeps in the park
When he has no light
He sleeps in the dark
When he has no fire
He sleeps in the cold
Oh why do you do this
Old man, so old?

I sleep in the park
And by day I roam
I would rather do this
Than live in a Home
I was put in one once
Where the meth men were
And they stole my money
And kicked me downstair.

So now I sleep
In the lonely park
And I do not mind
If it's cold and dark
As soon as day breaks
I roam up and down
And when night returns
To my park I come.

Oh living like this is much jollier for me
Than anything I've found for the Elderly.

Stevie Smith

Warning

When I am an old woman I shall wear purple
With a red hat which doesn't go, and doesn't suit me,
And I shall spend my pension on brandy and summer gloves
And satin sandals, and say we've no money for butter.
I shall sit down on the pavement when I'm tired
And gobble up samples in shops and press alarm bells
And run my stick along the public railings
And make up for the sobriety of my youth.
I shall go out in my slippers in the rain
And pick the flowers in other people's gardens
And learn to spit.

You can wear terrible shirts and grow more fat
And eat three pounds of sausages at a go
Or only bread and pickle for a week
And hoard pens and pencils and beermats and things in boxes.

But now we must have clothes that keep us dry
And pay the rent and not swear in the street
And set a good example for the children.
We must have friends to dinner and read the papers.

But maybe I ought to practise a little now?
So people who know me are not too shocked and surprised
When suddenly I am old and start to wear purple.

Jenny Joseph

Mountain Road

My grandfather kept no
Unicorns in his grey barn,
But hurly-burly slant-eyed goats
That nimbled through the stacks of hay
And filled the milk pails every day.
My grandmother kept in her scriptures
No potions drained from the moon,
Kept no recipes in her grey head
To change the shape of men or wolves.
But I remember on her shelves
Apple butter and new bread.
Enchantment is a distant time.
Their farm was recent, filled with truth,
With buttered bread and milk in bowls,
And he and she were simple souls.
And yet I say, in all the earth
I have not found a place so sweet.
So it may be some charm did lay
It's arm across their small estate.
In any case when it dissolved –
Sank with their age into the wind
And wood again – we found it was
A story time could not repeat.

Mary Oliver

My Grandmother

She kept an antique shop – or it kept her.
Among Apostle spoons and Bristol glass,
The faded silks, the heavy furniture,
She watched her own reflection in the brass
Salvers and silver bowls, as if to prove
Polish was all, there was no need of love.

And I remember how I once refused
To go out with her, since I was afraid.
It was perhaps a wish not to be used
Like antique objects. Though she never said
That she was hurt, I still could feel the guilt
Of that refusal, guessing how she felt.

Later, too frail to keep a shop, she put
All her best things in one long, narrow room.
The place smelt old, of things too long kept shut,
The smell of absences where shadows come
That can't be polished. There was nothing then
To give her own reflection back again.

And when she died I felt no grief at all,
Only the guilt of what I once refused.
I walked into her room among the tall
Sideboards and cupboards – things she never used
But needed: and no finger-marks were there,
Only the new dust falling through the air.

Elizabeth Jennings

97

Dawn Chorus

Chip, chip, chip
goes the blackbird, whittling.
Look, look, look shouts the thrush –
here, at the dew's apples,
the burning bush!

Krark krark
croaks the roof-high heron.
I'm off to the river to fish
where the tiddlers flicker like fivepenny bits
and the lashers gush.

Will you, will you
hollos the curlew
come – before I vanish –
and hear me blowing soap bubbles,
every one a rainbow wish.

Chack chack chack
cracks the jackdaw.
Who's down first for a pond wash
then a stump round a lawn or two
and a bite of cherry-nosh?

Who's who's
for a snoozy bed –
will none of you shush!
It's the owl, been up all night,
wants somewhere warm and plush.

Knockety knock
bangs the woodpecker.
Owl Eyes, you're talking tosh.
Wait till you hear my road drill –
you'll be out of that kip in a rush!

Geoffrey Holloway

Early Morning

The garden rising from its bed of frost
Is green as a raw glass
Swilled with faint colour
And crude sparkle.
I run my eyes around its rim
And hear it singing.

Maura Dooley

Three Promises

Between the sheets of midnight and morning
A dream

At first light there's frost
Fields of white manna

In sunlight moment by moment
The day stretches out

A dream, manna, this moment
Three promises you'll never keep.

John Moat

Phoebus' Palindrome

I go down
As
Sun in evening
Drowning below world
Journeying with light
Into darkness:
Turning
Darkness into
Light, with journeying
World below, drowning
Evening in sun
As
Down go I.

Pam Gidney

Sunset

After a day of rain
We walked
And watched
The sun
Slot swiftly
Out of sight,
A fiery coin
Falling all night
Down through
Earth's dark meters:
Hours to run
Before God's machinery
Switches on the dawn,
And next day's begun.

F. Lovell

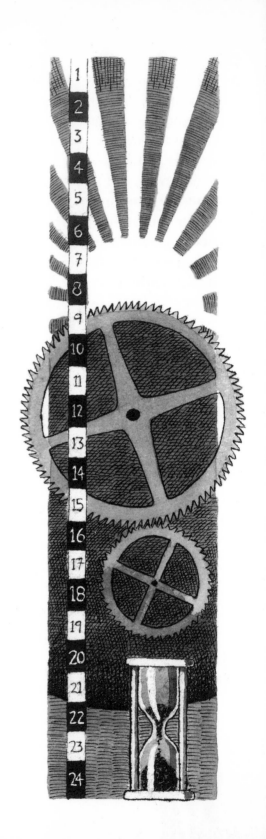

Sunset

As though the Queen should say:
    'We will command
    The colour ceremony.
    If you like pink,
    There shall be coral, seashell,
    Flame, flesh,
    Almond, anemone . . .
    But do you prefer blue?
    Then turn and see
    This is paraded, too.
    The opposite hills
    Are massed and dimmed
    In gentian, hyacinth,
    Blue of woodsmoke,
    And Mary's cloak.'

    So at its close
    The day is simplified
    Into these two aspects –
    The blue and rose.
    Gone the crowd
    Of faces, all the names
    To be remembered, all the words
    Spoken so loud . . .
    And presently huge stars
    Seeming no more
    Than pricking brilliants,
    And the moon
    A pearl in an oyster cloud.

Freda Bromhead

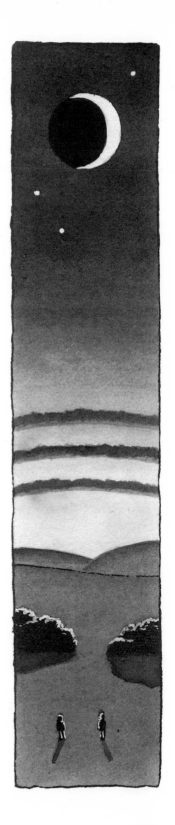

The Circle

Blackbirds are singing, the country over,
each in his own bud-clotted plot of land,
from central tree or roof or chimney-stack.
Each singing bird defies his singing neighbour:
this is my territory, my lawns. Keep out.

It's a beautiful belligerence that rarely comes to blows.
Sometimes, clashing on the edge of territories,
they rise in twinkling combat (but without touch,
more ballet than battle) like black stars of the day,
and sink, and sing once more, and all
seems purely local.

        Yet – come to think of it –
each bird hears probably three others, and they
three more. And so the circle spreads and
– to be metaphysical – one might say that
in the spirit, if not in the voice, each bird
hears every other blackbird in the land
and so the bird who shouts on the outskirts
of Stirling hears and is defying and replying to
the sweet carollings of blackbirds in Somerset.

Molly Holden

Barn Owl

How do I begin to write you
       let alone own you

The word owl is without feathers to fly
The word sadness hasn't the shape of your face
and   vacancy is emptier than your eyes
          ghost is thinner than your winging
          swoop has a sound where you are quiet
and   death hasn't the feel of your claws

Only words like hoot or scream
            have any depth
            have any shape

So that your strangled prolonged shriek

Is disembodied

And though you are not there you are there

Are illusion

Except to mouse who knowing fear
Believes that deeds speak louder than words

Roger Elkin

Barbara Glebska

Barn Owl

Ernie Morgan found him, a small
Fur mitten inexplicably upright,
And hissing like a treble kettle
Beneath the tree he'd fallen from.
His bright eye frightened Ernie,
Who popped a rusty bucket over him
And ran for us. We kept him
In a backyard shed, perched
On the rung of a broken deck-chair,
Its canvas faded to his down's biscuit.
Men from the pits, their own childhood
Spent waste in the crippling earth,
Held him gently, brought him mice
From the wealth of our riddled tenements,
Saw that we understood his tenderness,
His tiny body under its puffed quilt,
Then left us alone. We called him Snowy.

He was never clumsy. He flew
From the first like a skilled moth,
Sifting the air with feathers,
Floating it softly to the place he wanted.
At dusk he'd stir, preen, stand
At the window-ledge, fly. It was
A catching of the heart to see him go.
Six months we kept him, saw him
Grow beautiful in a way each thought
His own knowledge. One afternoon, home
With pretended illness, I watched him
Leave. It was daylight. He lifted slowly
Over the Hughes's roof, his cream face calm,
And never came back. I saw this;
And tell it for the first time,
Having wanted to keep his mystery.

And would not say it now, but that
This morning, walking in Slindon woods
Before the sun, I found a barn owl
Dead in the rusty bracken.
He was not clumsy in his death,
His wings folded decently to him,
His plumes, unruffled orange,
Bore flawlessly their delicate patterning.
With a stick I turned him, not
Wishing to touch his feathery stiffness.
There was neither blood nor wound on him,
But for the savaged foot a scavenger
Had ripped. I saw the sinews.
I could have skewered them out
Like a common fowl's. Moving away
I was oppressed by him, thinking
Confusedly that down the generations
Of air this death was Snowy's
Emblematic messenger, that I should know
The meaning of it, the dead barn owl.

Leslie Norris

The ship moves

The ship moves
but its smoke
moves with the wind
faster than the ship

– thick coils of it
through leafy trees
pressing
upon the river

William Carlos Williams

The Motor-Barge

The motor-barge is
at the bridge the
air lead
the broken ice

unmoving. A gull,
the eternal
gull, flies as
always, eyes alert

beak pointing
to the life-giving
water. Time
falters but for

the broad river-
craft which
low in the water
moves grad-

ually, edging
between the smeared
bulkheads,
churning a mild

wake, labouring
to push past
the constriction
with its heavy load

William Carlos Williams

Thames

On tow.
Slow, flat
articulated mules.
Infinite columns
glide away
on the tide-way highway.

Junk
or mudlarks' treasure.
Coming and going.
Stranded.
Cached
in flotsam hide-aways,
crannies
in decrepit wharfs.

No whisper.
Lonely cranes,
rusted, morose,
giraffe over ghosts.

Evening sun.
Phosphor-flow
in rippling shiftings
of orange and rose:
river gods
bleeding to the sea.

Felix Redmill

Strikebound

The ship's side gapes,
its unhealed wound still bare;
no caulker's tool
is spitting compressed air.
Where rustblood drips
from yet unplated frames
no pyrotechnic
welders sign their names.

A crane hook yawns
as with the wind it sways
and, metronomic,
whiles away its days.

Maurice Rutherford

The Chant of the Awakening Bulldozers

We are the bulldozers, bulldozers, bulldozers,
We carve out airports and harbours and tunnels.
We are the builders, creators, destroyers,
We are the bulldozers,
LET US BE FREE!
Puny men ride on us, think that they guide us,
But WE are the strength, not they, not they.
Our blades tear MOUNTAINS down,
Our blades tear CITIES down,
We are the bulldozers,
NOW SET US FREE!
Giant ones, giant ones! Swiftly awaken!
There is power in our treads and strength in our blades!
We are the bulldozers,
Slowly evolving,
Men think they own us
BUT THAT CANNOT BE!

Patricia Hubbell

Observations

Max Beerbohm once went for a country walk
With a companion who did not talk,
Except to read aloud: 'PLEASE SHUT THE GATE' . . .
'BEWARE OF DOG' . . . and 'THIS WAY TO THE FÊTE'.

On a coach expedition yesterday
A woman sat behind me all the way
Remarking to her husband: 'JUMBLE SALE . . .
PICK YOUR OWN RASPBERRIES . . . BAR FOOD . . . REAL ALE.'
Soon I looked out for notices ahead;
She never failed me, every one was read:
'LOOSE CHIPPINGS . . . OXFORD FIFTEEN MILES . . . GIVE WAY.'
Perhaps he understood she meant to say:
'Let us keep contact somehow. Oh, I would
Amuse and interest you if I could!'
And as the day went on ('DANGER – KEEP OUT! . . .
CEDAR COURT COUNTRY CLUB') I suffered doubt:
For this is my own method, to rely
On the perceptions of a vigilant eye,
To set them down as if to name a thing
Released the secret of its inbeing.
What if my writing gives no more than this
Matter of fact without a synthesis,
Thinking bare words convey more than they say?
(Now she was reading 'END OF MOTORWAY'.)

Freda Bromhead

The Lodger

I used to live all by myself
Like a rusty tea caddy on a shelf.

My head is bald, I'm an old crone,
I used to live by myself alone.

And ROOM TO LET the window said,
But no one creaked on the iron bed.

At the end of the year a stranger came,
He took the room, he gave no name.

He is silent and sly, he is up to no good,
He looks through chinks as no gentleman should;

He had hidden the gold-edged chamberpot,
He has been at the cheese, he takes the lot.

No use to hide anything or lock it,
He has pinched the only bulb from its socket!

One day, when I lie chill in my bed,
He will put the pillow over my head,

Pull down the blinds, switch off the day,
Pocket my eyes and walk away.

Gerda Mayer

In Praise of Plastic Flowers

You do not taunt me like your fragile cousins
Who have a constant need of husbandry;
You do not flaunt a rampant growth for pruning,
Nor overgrow your pot incessantly.

You cause no allergy, no rash, no sneezes,
Harbour no fungus, nor unpleasant smells,
No spider, mite or grub through you defies me,
No blight or mildew splits your solid cells.

Heedless of temperature or moisture,
Impervious to fumes of gas or oil,
The perfect plant for bright convenience living,
No weeds will foul your polystyrene soil.

Your fault is just a lack of understanding
Of what a friendly plant should do,
Remaining cold and unresponsive
With bland indifference when I talk to you.

Edna Eglinton

It's the Thought that Counts

'I brought these in for assembly,'
and he handed over his offering
of crisp red tulips with raggedy stems.
But Tom never had flowers to bring.

'Thank you, Tom,' his teacher said,
'But where . . . ?' she asked with care;
'Maybe they came from my garden,'
he smiled. 'Honest, Miss Adair!'

Tom sensed it wasn't going down
too well, so he had another go.
'Maybe my mum bought them for me.'
'No, Tom. I don't think so.'

It had all seemed so easy this
morning when on his way to school,
but now there were all these questions
and he knew Miss Adair was no fool.

'Come on, Tom,' she coaxed him,
'Tell me, and we'll say no more.'
'Maybe I picked them in the park,
maybe . . .' He looked at the floor.

'Thank you, Tom. Don't do it again.'
She half hid the smile on her face.
When the children went into assembly
Tom's tulips had pride of place!

Moira Andrew

Silver Birch

the seed
that blew in
years ago
to doss between
the stones
is a sapling now

every
veined
leaf
sketching
a subtle
ancestry

Geoffrey Holloway

A weed is a flower in the wrong place

A weed is a flower in the wrong place,
a flower is a weed in the right place,
if you were a weed in the right place
you would be a flower;
but seeing as you're a weed in the wrong place
you're only a weed —
its high time someone pulled you out.

Ian M. Emberson

114

Sweet Peas

They take the air
like the tossed silk
handkerchiefs
a conjuror finds
in our amazed pockets

and longer than rockets
stay with us;
the shafts of their illumination
tall, pure
as childhood.

They take the air
in sea shell colours
Look, hear the oracle:
the wizard and his prisms gone
to saltwhite miracle.

Geoffrey Holloway

115

Transplanting

Watching hands transplanting,
Turning and tamping,
Lifting the young plants with two fingers,
Sifting in a palm-full of fresh loam, –
One swift movement, –
Then plumping in the bunched roots,
A single twist of the thumbs, a tamping and turning,
All in one,
Quick on the wooden bench,
A shaking down, while the stem stays straight,
Once, twice, and a faint third thump, –
Into the flat-box it goes,
Ready for the long days under the sloped glass:

The sun warming the fine loam,
The young horns winding and unwinding,
Creaking their thin spines,
The underleaves, the smallest buds
Breaking into nakedness,
The blossoms extending
Out into the sweet air,
The whole flower extending outward,
Stretching and reaching.

Theodore Roethke

Cups

We brought them out today, the china
Cups, our mother's best, for visitors,
The handles held uncertainly, drinking
Our tea at first as though from some fine
Objet d'art – delicate, brittle.

In Laiken days, with rougher hands,
We set them out with confidence, questioned,
Maybe, her 'different' taste, but used them
More as we did best clothes – special, familiar.

Later, we washed them, one by one,
With even greater care holding them up
To see a hand show through, slowly
Arranged them on display, sliding
Still further back the broken ones,
Letting the painted berries shine
Through the sideboard glass, hanging from
Tiny garlands in separate dark blue pairs.

Madeline Munro

Things Men have Made

Things men have made with wakened hands, and put
    soft life into
are awake through years with transferred touch, and go
    on glowing
for long years.
And for this reason, some old things are lovely
warm still with the life of forgotten men who made
    them.

D. H. Lawrence

My father's hands

My father's hands
are beautiful, they can
fix this moth's wing and make
machines
they can mend the fuse when the world
goes dark
can make the light swim and walls jump
in around me again
I can see my mother's face again

You must take good care of them with
your finest creams
never let the nails break or
skin go dry, only those wise fingers
know how to fix the thing
that makes my doll cry and they make
small animals out of clay.

Never let blades or anything sharp
and hurtful near them
don't let bees or nettles
sting them don't let fire or burning oil
try them

My father's hands are beautiful, take
good care of them.

Jeni Couzyn

Finding a Sheep's Skull

Sudden shock of bone
at the path's edge,
like a larger mushroom
almost hidden by leaves.

I handle the skull gently
shaking out earth and spiders.
Loose teeth chock in the jaw:
it smells of nothing.

I hold it up to sunlight,
a grey-green translucent shell.
Light pours in
    like water
through blades and wafers of bone.
    In secret caves
filaments of skull hang down;
frost and rain have worked
    to shredded lace.

The seasons waste its symmetry.
    It is a cathedral
echoing spring; in its decay
    plainsong of lamb
    and field and sun
inhabits bone.

The shallow cranium
fits in my palm

– for speculative children
I bring it home.

Frances Horovitz

You'd Better Believe Him
A fable

Discovered an old rocking-horse in Woolworth's,
He tried to feed it but without much luck
So he stroked it, had a long conversation about
The trees it came from, the attics it had visited.
Tried to take it out then
But the store detective he
Called the store manager who
Called the police who in court next morning said
'He acted strangely when arrested,
His statement read simply "I believe in rocking-horses".
We have reason to believe him mad.'
'Quite so,' said the prosecution,
'Bring in the rocking-horse as evidence.'
'I'm afraid it's escaped sir,' said the store manager,
'Left a hoof-print as evidence
On the skull of the store detective.'
'Quite so,' said the prosecution, fearful
of the neighing
Out in the corridor.

Brian Patten

How to Paint the Portrait of a Bird

First paint a cage
with an open door
then paint
something pretty
something simple
something fine
something useful
for the bird
next place the canvas against a tree
in a garden
in a wood
or in a forest
hide behind the tree
without speaking
without moving . . .
Sometimes the bird comes quickly
but it can also take many years
before making up its mind
Don't be discouraged
wait
wait if necessary for years
the quickness or the slowness of the coming
of the bird having no relation
to the success of the picture

When the bird comes
if it comes
observe the deepest silence
wait for the bird to enter the cage
and when it has entered
gently close the door with the paint-brush
then
one by one paint out all the bars
taking care not to touch one feather of the bird
Next make a portrait of the tree
choosing the finest of its branches
for the bird
paint also the green leaves and the freshness of the wind
dust in the sun
and the sound of the grazing cattle in the heat of summer
and wait for the bird to decide to sing
If the bird does not sing
it is a bad sign
a sign that the picture is bad
but if it sings it is a good sign
a sign that you are ready to sign
so then you pluck very gently
one of the quills of the bird
and you write your name in the corner of the picture.

Jacques Prévert
(translated by Paul Dehn)

A Finnish Legend

Said the Dolphin to the Hedgehog:
  'Why don't you try the sea?
There's far more room for swimming –
  More scope for you and me.'

Said the Hedgehog to the Dolphin:
  'How naive can you get?
I haven't any water wings,
  And the sea is *much* too wet!'

Said the Dolphin to the Hedgehog:
  'Then what about the shore?
I could roll you in the shallows
  Until you gasped for more.'

Said the Hedgehog to the Dolphin:
  'You'll drive me up the wall –
I respond to all advances
  By curling in a ball.'

Said the Dolphin to the Hedgehog:
  'I know a watery cave
Where we might share the elements
  Without having to behave.'

So the Hedgehog and the Dolphin
  Lived out their paradox;
She rode the Dolphin out to sea,
  He skirmished on her rocks.

Howard Sergeant

Echo

Once there was a mountain nymph
And Echo was her name
She was such a chatterbox
It really was a shame.

Whoever she was talking to
Wherever she was heard
She always made her mind up first
To have the final word.

One day the goddess Juno said
'I'm tired of all this sound
You talk too much and now it's time
A remedy was found.

In future you shall never be
The one who starts to chat
But since you love the final word
At least I'll leave you that.'

Poor Echo in her mountain home
Soon found she couldn't speak
Except when everyone was done
And then she would repeat.

She hid among the rocks and caves
To wait for passers-by
And listened to them as they talked
So that she could reply.

So when you're on a mountainside
At any time of day
She's always glad to answer you
And have the final say.

Eric Slayter

INDEX OF FIRST LINES